SALFORD

Yesterday AND Today

BY

Cliff Hayes

in association with the

Published by
Memories
222 King Road
Old Trafford
Manchester M16 OJA

© Cliff Hayes

Cliff Hayes

ISBN1 899181 84 9

Published in association with

Manchester EveningNews

Printed by
MFP Design & Print
Longford Trading Estate
Thomas Street Stretford
Manchester
M32 0JT
Tel: 0161 864 4540

Produced by NPS
28 Bedford Road
Firswood
Manchester M16 OJA
Telephone 0161 862 9399

Other books by the author:
Manchester Yesterday & Today
This was Trafford Park
Old Trafford
Salford Docks
Britain in old photographs - Stretford
Britain in old photographs - Chorlton
Postcards of Old Salford

ACKNOWLEDGEMENTS

To Jed McCann for his help, and for photographs needed to complete the today's photography. To Ted Gray for additional postcards of Old Salford, and helpful advice, as always. To Gordon Coltas (Locofotos) for digging out all his Agecroft and Patricroft photos and giving permission for them to be used. Thanks to Harry Scarsbrook for his old photos. To Vince Gillibrand for the Ordsall hall and Crescent photographs. Thanks to all the staff of the Local History Library in Peel Park, especially to Tim Ashworth, for permission to included the racecourse photos. To the staff at The Heritage Centre, at Salford Quays - especially to Ken for the loan of the pictures of Salford Docks.

INTRODUCTION

RECORDING the 'today' part of history is not as easy as it sounds. You take a picture today, and by the time your photograph is developed, that view is 'yesterday'. It could be that someone has made single yellow lines, double, a well known shop has closed and become a charity shop, or more parking meters have appeared. Time moves on, with or without us.

As we stand on the threshold of a millennium, I thought that it would be good to compare views from yesterday with the same view today, showing Salford as it was, and in doing so, record, for a future generations, how the place looks today. And as I have already said, views and photographs of Salford in 1998 will themselves be Salford's 'past' all too soon.

So, I hope you enjoy the comparisons, look for the differences, and marvel at the similarities in . . .

'This is how you do it, grandad'. The Author Cliff receives re-training from his new assistant (and grand-daughter) Hannah.

Salford Yesterday and Today.

A busy scene for the races at Castle Irwell over 90 years ago. Will horse racing come back to the area?

Sacred Trinity Church, at the junction of Chapel St. and Blackfriars Rd. Above we see it c. 1938 and below, today. Built in early 1630s and opened in 1635, it had been Humphrey Booth who had pushed for a Chapel of Ease in Salford (hence Chapel St.) and who paid most towards the cost of building. Now a study centre and church offices and well looked after.

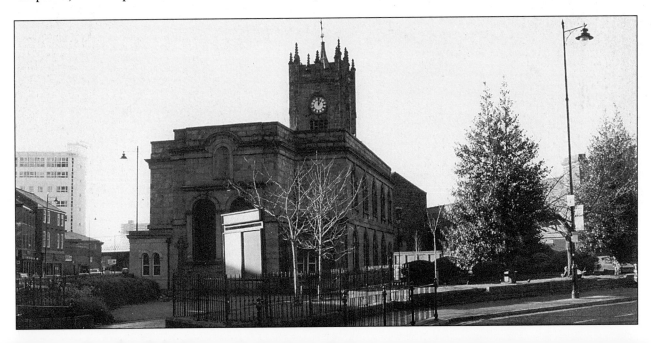

Sacred Trinity Church, thought to be the only one in Britain with that dedication, got the nickname the "Flat Iron" church because of the markets held on the spare land adjacent to the church. There was sold flat or smoothing irons, new and second hand, and the market's area was also shaped like a flat-iron. Above we see a busy market a 100 years ago and below a close up of the church today showing the work done when it was re-built in 1753.

Chapel Street, Salford was one of the first areas in the town to become built up, and later the first slum area of Salford. Because it was near the centre of Salford it contained many public houses and Inns. Above our view shows the street in 1878 and three of the buildings are pubs. Below we see the Chapel of the United Reform Church, built in 1819.

The triangle of streets that is Gravel Lane, Chapel Street and Greengate WAS once Salford's town centre and where the Town Cross and stocks once stood. We see an engraving above, from about 1830. Bonny Prince Charlie was blessed here by the Salford vicar, Dr. John Cousins. John Wesley himself preached here after being thrown out of Trinity church. Very little goes on here today except for parking cars. That history is still there, under those car parks. It's a shame that there is not some sort of more permanent reminder of those stirring events.

The old centre of Salford, the area which was once at the very heart of the community, is now nothing more than an open area of car parking. Above we see the 'Bull's Head Inn', on Greengate as it was in 1907. Once the oldest public house in the area (some say in England) it closed and stood empty until a fire sealed its fate in 1935. It was offered to the Council as a museum for £1. Today that very same view shows, you've guessed it, just a car park.

Greengate, Salford was a very busy and bustling area, as our photo from 1930, above, shows. It was a lived in community, and right at the heart of Old Salford Town. Manchester centre seems to be getting a lot of re-generation money, I wonder if this City centre could attract any of the flats, city centre housing, redevelopment that is around today. They certainly have the open space to re-build if they wanted to, as we see in our today picture below.

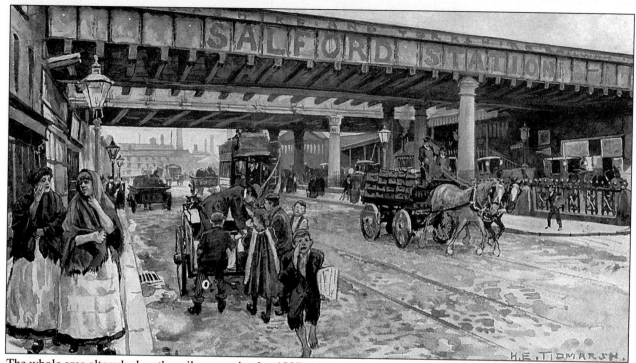

The whole area altered when the railways arrived c. 1837. Above we see a drawing by H.E. Tidmarsh of Salford Railway Station, looking down New Bailey St, a century ago. At one time The Lancashire and Yorkshire Railway Co, stopped the East Lancs railway running into Manchester Victoria station and their train would terminate here and horse drawn cabs would rush businessmen into 'town'. Below we see the view today, but taken from over the lights in Bloom St.

Chapel Street continuation, looking out towards Windsor Bridge. The Roman Catholic Cathedral of St. John the Evangelist dominated the right hand side of the road. It still does today, as we see below. Bexley Sq. is in the right foreground, behind the first gas-light and tram wire pole. People do not walk to the shops much these days and this has meant the death of many of the old main shopping streets. If you can't park outside the shop many people won't shop there.

Bexley Sq. Salford became the centre of the City when the cross was taken down and the Town Hall built here. It too has been the scene of many exciting and important scenes of the past including the Means Test riots, and unemployed rallies. The square is named after Lord Bexley, who was Chancellor to the Duchy of Lancaster, when he laid the foundation stone to Salford Town Hall in 1825. Above is the view just over a century ago, and below the square today. The Court House, that was the Town Hall, has open days once a year and are well worth looking out for.

13

Regent Road, looking down from the junction of Cross Lane and Trafford Road. Above we see it as it was in about 1916. There are a lot of uniforms on our picture and even one poor soldier on crutches on the right hand side. This area was really very busy and thronged with shops and people. Today as we see below it is still a busy area but with cars, rushing to get through Salford and on to the motorway system.

Eccles New Road, Salford, and we are looking the other way from the previous picture. We have also moved on a few years as our Yesterday photo above is from c 1929. The Ship Hotel is on the corner and a policeman, all dressed in white is on crossing duty, but he has more pedestrians than traffic to control. Below we see the same spot today, with Salford Court House on the right, (they need a proper sign on that place), and the Spire Pub away on the left.

The very bottom of Cross Lane, looking over into Trafford Road, pictured above in c. 1907. The Stowell Memorial Church is on the left, consecrated on May 14th, 1869 in memory of Rev. Hugh Stowell who died in 1865 after 40 years of preaching in Salford. It cost £8,000, even then, and could seat 700 worshippers. You can see in close up the Regent Theatre, renamed the Palace in 1919, and from the names over the doors you are informed that it was also the Assembly Rooms, the entrance to those being bottom right hand corner. Today this same spot is the roundabout at the end of the M602 and though the 150ft spire is still there all else has gone.

Cross Lane, Salford, taken from Trafford Road on an Edwardian postcard. That's the wall of the church on the left and The Ship Inn, middle left, of our view. The Regent Theatre next to it opened on Sept 2nd, 1895 and could seat over 1,700 people. Houdini escaped from a locked coffin here in 1904. It was for a time two picture houses, then went went back to live shows after one burnt out in 1941. All the top stars of the day played at this theatre, Joseph Locke, Frank Randle, Robb Wilton, this theatre had seen them all. You can just make out the 'barracks' further up Cross Lane. Today's view below shows roads and work units and some new housing.

Cross Lane junction with Eccles New Road, seen in close-up from the early 1920's. The Ship Hotel on the left of the picture was a notorious drinking den, and the theatre next door, opened as the Regent Theatre, now bears the name, Palace. Note the tramlines in the cobbles. This junction was one of the most intricate in Britain. Called a 'Grand Union' it had two lines turning left and right from each direction and two lines going straight across. When the M602 round-about was being made the lines were carefully lifted and are now at Crich Tram Museum. Today's Ship Hotel is not quite on the site of the old one, it's further up Cross Lane as we see below.

A close-up of the barracks and drill hall on Cross Lane, taken around 1910. As you can see from the gate the 7th and 8th Lancashire Fusiliers were in residence at the time. Today there is not a trace of the imposing building, that was pulled down in the late 1960's, and, as we see below houses stand on the spot today.

Cross Lane has changed more than any other main road in Salford. Once it was one of the busiest thoroughfares in the town, it had a theatre at both ends, the military barracks (drill hall), and the markets were there. Above we see cattle, from the near-by Cattle Market, crossing the road in front of the aptly named Cattle Market Hotel on a view from a century ago. The same spot is seen below on our today photograph.

The Windsor Bridge end of Cross Lane had the Hippodrome Theatre, opened March 1904. Our view above, shows that theatre just after it opened, seat prices starting at just 2d. Later the name was changed to the Windsor Theatre and it closed down in 1956. The oblisk showing on the right is the only bit of our photograph still there. Erected in honour of Oliver Heywood, the banker, who used so much of his money to help the poor and needy in Salford. It is still there today in the car park of MacDonald's drive through, as we see right.

Bolton Road, Irlams O' Th' Height, seen above from a postcard of the late Edwardian period. The name of the area produces many problems for outsiders with the apostrophies, and the plural Irlams yet singular Height. A postman once told me about half of the local mail had the address mis-spelt. The Heights seemed easiest. Those houses on the left are still there today and St. John's church in the distance.

Langworthy Road, Seedley, says the caption to our postcard above from the 1920s. Langworthy Road was a mixture of shops and private houses at the time. The road was named after Edward Riley Langworthy for his work as Councillor and founder of Libraries in Salford. The Langworthy Hotel on the right is still there, as we see on our today picture below but boarded up and unused.

Two 1960s pictures here and, though they may seem modern to some of us pensioners, they are from over 30 years ago. Above we see Silk Street, down at the bottom of Adelphi St. looking towards Great Clowes St. and the gigantic flats they built there to house the people moved from Greengate and Trinity wards. Right, are again those flats, towering over one of the factories that dominated the area of Adelphi St. and Cannon St.

Regent Road was always one of the main approaches to Salford. It was also (unfortunately) one of the roads you had to use if you wanted to get from Warrington or Widnes into Manchester. Above we see Regent Road, looking from Ordsall Lane and looking away from town, as it appeared in 1905. Did everything really have to go? Did the demolition have to be so complete? It really is hard to believe that we are looking a the same spot some 90 years later below.

Ellor St., Hanky Park is the caption on our 1950s picture above. 'Hanky Park' has become a rallying cry for 'Old Salford'. If ever an area was changed out of all recognition, if ever a community was decimated by modernisation which swept aside all traces of the old, it was here. Hanky Park got its name from Hankinson St. which was one of the busier and larger streets in the 'Park'. All that is left of Ellor St. is the recycling bins and a car park as we see below.

Looking down Ellor Street towards St. Paul's Church and Hankinson St in the early 1950s. The street received its fame from Walter Greenwood and his novel 'Love on The Dole' which exposed the Means Test for the harsh authority that it was. Where the shops on the right, above, were is now the middle of the Salford Precinct and W. H. Smiths and Marks & Spencer's today as we see below.

Peel Park & The Langworthy Gallery, Salford said the caption on our above photograph from a century ago. It's taken from the back of the Museum showing how it looks out over the park. Today as we see below it's the other side that draws our attention, for it contains the Local History Library (always worth a visit), the Art Gallery, and the unique, Lark Hill Place; the reproduction street that contains so many memories of Old Salford.

A photograph from September 1963 when work began on the widening of Salford Crescent. The disruption to traffic then was horrendous, but people put up with it with far more grace and decorum than they would today. Luckily there is not a lot of disruption on the Crescent today and it forms one of the main arterial roads in and out of Manchester, as we see in our today photograph from the same spot.

Be honest now. As you drive along the Crescent do you think of the River Irwell that flows along below all the bustle of city Traffic each day? Above we see the bend in the river that flows alongside the Crescent from a 1937 view, Salford Royal and St. Philips and the cathedral spires show up against the skyline. Below we see the river today, but viewed from the other direction.. The far side of the river bank was where they filmed 'Hobson's Choice' all those years ago.

Trams on the Crescent c. 1919, looking towards the Cathedral and Bexley Square. The superior view over Peel Park did make the houses here very desirable: "As Will Mossop said". I wonder if the trams will return to the Crescent? It's wide enough for trams to run in the 'bus lanes', as our today picture below shows.

(Locofotos).

Salford once had two major railway engine depots in its area. There was Agecroft Motive Power Depot (shed) which closed down on 22nd October, 1966, and Patricroft which hung on until the end of steam, a year later. Above we see the line-up outside Agecroft in 1948 and saddle-tank 51230 with other tank engines steamed up and ready for local work. Below we see a close up of tank engine 51207, again with a stove-pipe chimney, inside the shed in the summer of 1961.

(Locofotos).

Agecroft colliery had its own engines and shed. There were three engines in the 50s and 60s 'Agecroft 1', '2' and '3'. Above we see 'Agecroft 2' backing full coal wagons to the coal tipper on the 4th February 1973. Below we see No. 2 hurrying back to the shed at the end of the shift. Can you just make out B.R. 40 diesel (Whistler) no. 324 passing on the line which ran past the colliery. I've not included any today shots to get in more of the wonderful yesterday photos.

Agecroft M.P.D. provided a lot of the engines to work the local services out of Manchester Exchange and Manchester Victoria Stations. This meant that many engines were the smaller and older classes. Above we see side tank engine no. 47201 over the ash pit having dropped its fire after a hard day's work. There were some express engines and below we see L.M.S. Jubilee No. 45564 "New South Wales" and 42901 on shed on June 9th, 1963.

Patricroft Depot was the more important of the depots. It supplied engines for the Yorkshire and London trains out of Manchester Exchange Station. Its shed number was 10C and all engine 'shedded' there would carry that number on the bottom of their front boiler doors. Above we see Standard B.R. engine 73097 ready to begin its day's duties in the early 1960s. Below we see 47201 in storage waiting to be taken away for cutting up.

A horse drawn tram makes its way down Eccles New Road in 1894, over a 100 years ago. The age of electric travel and electric trams was still to come when our above photograph was taken. Horse power on rails was the latest thing and Salford was right there with the new technology. Trams are due back to Salford and Eccles and below we see the scene in 1998 as they re-lay tram lines down Eccles New Road. The tram will follow before the new millenium. (photo R. J. S. Wiseman).

It's over 50 years since the last electric tram ran in Salford. Above we see the last tram No. 350 ready to run the last route (the 70) for Salford on Monday night, on the 31st, March, 1947. The 70 ran from Salford Dock gates via Trafford Road, Cross Lane, Broad St and Frederick Rd to the Central depot. Below we see the inside of that tram on its very last journey, with the conductor and driver chatting to lucky passengers before starting on that very last journey.

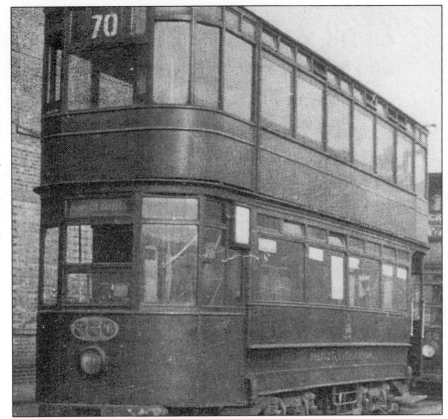

Trafford Road, Salford says the caption on our 1905 postcard. It's Ordsall really, an area that had a very strong identity that started to really build up after the docks opened in 1894. The tram power wires were carried on very ornate posts down the middle of the road, which was bustling and busy with shoppers. Not so today as our picture below shows. Shopping streets have been wiped out in favour of supermarkets and shopping centres. Is it really what we want, or what we are told we want?

Trafford Road again but lower down, towards the dock gates, is the view on our yesterday postcard above, from c. 1905 That's Custom House on the right, and the Salisbury Public House just further up the road. Most of the people on the picture seem to be dockers going into work, must have been dinner time. Everyone went home for their dinner (a cooked one) in those days. At least you can still get something to eat round here today. What with Starvin Marvin, Fatty Arbuckle and Frankie and Benny you would never go hungry.

Corner shops were the life-blood of the community, giving 'tick', advice, and the odd pint of port and sherry for weddings and funerals. Above we see Lizzie Fidler cleaning the step of her off-licence on the corner of West Park St., and Ruby St., Ordsall, in the 1950's. Ruby Street has gone, the nearest off licence I can find is the Welcome Inn (below), on Robert Hall St., Ordsall. Hall manufactured fire hoses that saved many lives a century ago. His factory was in Ordsall.

The Dock Gates, Trafford Road, seen above on a 1950s photograph, from the Manchester Ship Canal Co's archives. It also shows how near the ships were to the main road. Working docks have a magical aura about them, knowing that people and vessels arrive and leave to and from every corner of the world. Below we see the dock gates today and there is a preservation order on them. I think that some wording should be put on them and if the words Manchester Docks still rankles as much as it did 100 years ago, maybe we could cheat, just a little, and put Salford Docks across the top.

Manchester Races it may have been called but we all know they were in Salford. Above we see an aerial photograph of the course. To help you place things, that is the Racecourse Hotel halfway up the picture on the left. Salford had the flat racing and hurdles courses separate, jumping being on the inside. Horse racing started here in 1846 and after a spell down by the docks (New Barns) settled here at Castle Irwell for the second and final time in 1902 and lasted until 1963. Below we see a view of the stands and racecourse taken from Littleton Road bridge. (Photo by V. Aspery).

Above we see a view of the racecourse, taken from New Church Corporation flats in 1964. Racing had been abandoned a year before and the course has lost its fences and hurdles, but the stables are still there, centre picture. This photograph was used by Castle Irwell Properties Ltd to try and pursuade Salford Council to give permission for houses to be built on the grounds, when they appealed on Feb. 23rd, 1965. That appeal was turned down and the Council went on to use it for student accommodation. Today, one of the few signs of the racecourse is the turnstile building seen below.

Poet's Corner was one of the landmark pubs in the Salford area. A Greenall Whitley establishment it stood on the corner of Broughton Road and Hough Lane. Above we see it as it was in the 1950s with the large corner window, later boarded up, and off-licence (bring your own jug) to the left. You can look in vain for the pub on our today picture below. That's the same corner, with Hough Lane off to the right, but for Poet's Corner, it's vanished, like so many other Salford landmarks.

Great Clowes Street, Lower Broughton, says the caption on our postcard above, from c. 1912. It shows, on the right the Victoria Theatre, and the Irwell Castle Hotel. The Victoria opened as a theatre on Monday Dec. 10, 1900, and the building went from cinema to live shows, to cinema right through until Saturday July 19th, 1958 when it closed. It opened as the Victoria Social Club (bingo hall) in 1973 and is still going today, as we see below. The hotel next door was stripped of its ornamental finery in the 1950s but the theatre didn't lose its ornate top until the mid 1970s.

The streets of Ordsall in June 1972, just before the last clearance of the area started. Already the high rise flats in the Tatton St. area have arrived but our view shows the old and the then new together. The flats are still there as we see on our today picture to the right, but the row upon row of back-to-back terrace housing has gone and we worry more about car parking space.

Above we see the Woolpack Inn, Pendleton, once one of the most famous and recognisable pubs in the area. That is Eccles Old Road away to the left and Bolton Road, the A6 to Th' Height on the right. It was owned by local brewers Walker & Homfray but was swept away in 1967 to make way for the underpass and roadway seen below. Our old picture above shows a drinking fountain where passers-by could get a drink of water on their travels and a horse trough where animals could drink while their masters were in the Woolpack.

A wonderful view over the lower Irwell valley, taken from near Pendleton Church. Agecroft pit and the power station feature strongly in our view. It is very hard to date the view but it is probably the early 1960s. After reading the novel 'Hobson's Choice', I can't help thinking of Henry Hobson when I look at this view. When he went off for a 'think' this is the area he roamed, though it's a lot more built up than in his day as we see from our today shot below.

Pendleton Town Hall and Parish Church, from a postcard of 1909 is shown above. The Town Hall was noted for some lovely stained glass windows that were taken away for 'safety' in 1939. I wonder where they are now? The town hall went, with so much else, in the A6 widening scheme of the 1960's but the church is still there.

Our today photo proves that and St. Thomas's (to give the church its proper title) dates from 1831, and is the Parish church of Pendleton.

Kersal Cell is one of the oldest buildings in Salford and once home to the Byrom family. The Hall we see above, on a view from a century ago, dates back to the 1600s. It has been altered many times before and since and has had many uses including a Country Club. Someone lives at 22 Whitewater Drive. Is it a council house or maybe a semi? No, it's Kersal Cell, a 16th century manor house built on the site of a monastic cell, as we see below, today. I wonder if the ghost of a grey monk still walks the place.

The streets of Salford have changed beyond all recognition over the last 30 years. The community spirit will take a lot more to break than moving the people out of the closed streets, but today everything is for the almighty motor car. Above shows June St. Oldfield Road area in March 1974, the donkey stoned steps and cobbled streets seem a fairly innocent place for our youngster to play. Below we see the traffic calming devices and sturdy fences that keep control today.

Salford has many forgotten heroes, many great stories that have died away and are forgotten. The one that bugs me most is the story of the Bible Christians and the start of modern-day vegetarianism. There is a book called "A Guiltless Feast" about them, available from your local library, which is a fascinating read. Their church was on King Street in the very heart of old Salford and it was there that their founder Rev, William Cowherd was buried. It was he who founded the meatless society; it was he who brought the Brotherton's into the fold and started the good work they went on to do. Where is he today? Under this car on a car park in Salford. The bodies were not moved when the old church was demolished and a car park created. Some of the headstones even stick out through the shale covering. Does this hero deserve this?

Some of the stones of the church are still knocking around, as our above photograph shows, but it is a shame that there is no reminder of this great organisation. Salford was the first council in the world to ever put on a Vegetarian Banquet, and no matter if you are for or against it, the fact should be recorded. On Queen St., shown in our picture below, once stood a great Sunday School, where the poor and illiterate of Salford were taught and given a chance to better themselves in the harsh world of the 1800s. All paid for by the Bible Christians.

Ordsall Hall, home of the Radcliffe Family for so many years, has had so many other uses over the years. A social club, a theological training college, and now a museum. It's good that Lord Egerton saved it from demolition a century ago and it's great the Salford took it over and the hall does much to teach us of the history of the area. Everyone should make the effort to visit, at least once a year, and all schools in Salford and Manchester should be made to visit. Above we see an unusual view from a century ago. It's what we now think of as the back of the hall, as you approach from Ordsall Lane, taken from Taylorson Street. Below we see the Hall as you see it today.

There is often something going on at Ordsall Hall. They re-inact family life for the Radcliffes, and make it easier to understand how they used to live. Above we see a demonstrator on on of those 'Open Days' while below we see a today view of the south wing of the hall, taken with the photographer's (Vince) back to Guy Fawkes St. They put on very good exhibitions there and change them three or four times a year so it's never the same when you visit. Do pop along and see them.

Trafford Road swing bridge, above in a view from the 1930s. The bridge built in 1893 was made to swing to let ships into number one to four docks that were further up river. It was 1905 before the engineers were able to successfully install a system where the tram wires and lines would fall back into place when the bridge swung. Note the two globe wickerwork baskets on the left of the bridge. These were used to tell ships it was safe to approach and which ship had right of way. Below we see the bridge today along with its new partner alongside and devoid of baskets.

Our above picture of the Trafford Road Swing bridge is only six years ago, 1993, but what changes have happened since then. There was still two way traffic on the bridge, and though the bridge hadn't swung for many years, the hazard lights, warning traffic that it was about to swing, are still there. So too are the baskets. Come on Salford Council, the baskets were taken away while the bridge was being repainted, we would like them (or replicas) back please. Stories of how workers would jump off buses and trams and rush on foot across the bridge when the baskets went up, so they wouldn't get bridged and lose quarter of an hour's pay, waiting for the bridge to swing back. They would jump on the bus or tram in front and it was decided that as long as you had a ticket you could do this. There were up to 70,000 people working in Trafford Park and most used public transport so there could be up to 20 buses and trams all waiting for the bridge to re-open.

It really is hard for those who never knew the docks, to imagine just how busy they were. Thousands of men worked there and another 500 women were employed either producing the paperwork that went with the business or feeding and watering the dockers and sailors. Above we see the paddle tug Irlam pulling a ship out of number nine dock, to turn it ready for its 40 mile journey to the open sea. There really is a large amount of open water round here as our today picture below shows, and the more use we make of it, the better we will appreciate it.

Above we see a 1950 view of the number eight dock of the Manchester Ship Canal Company's docks at Salford. Cattle, sheep (frozen and live), coal, carbon and lamp black; bananas and coconuts; animal hides, horns and bones; barrage balloons; trains and boats and planes; and once even Agecroft Hall, packed up bit by bit and sold to America, have passed through these docks. Our today picture is from the same spot. Although the Quay House Hotel looks as if it was converted from some previous use it is in fact brand new, as is the Holiday Inn on the far side of the dock.

Where once we had ships from all over the world tying up to load and unload their precious cargoes now we have companies sending faxes and E-mails to those very same far away places. Above we have a Greek ship from the 1950s and right the offices on that same dockside today.

The rejuvenation of Salford Docks has been a long hard process. Salford Quays didn't just spring to life from the rubble of the redundant docks. It took a lot of hard work and effort, something we should be mindful of as we visit the area. Those Fen Shui addicts among you will know of the benefits of water around your living or working environs, and you have to admit there is plenty of water around the offices and eateries at Salford Quays. Still, they have done a good job, and praise where praise is due. Above we see the new canal between no. 8 and 7 docks, while left is a nice photo of the cranes left as a reminder of the working docks. I think there should be a plaque on those cranes to the dockers, workers and sailors from Salford who gave their lives in the Second World War.

There is at the moment some doubt about the future of those two large cranes. We are told the cost of preserving them is too high. I do hope they survive.

The Lowry Centre, we couldn't get away without mentioning it, and here we show two views of it during construction. Above we see it from Trafford Wharf, the other side of the Canal, in February 1999 and below from the Salford side in 1998. They say it will be ready for March 2000 and is on time. it will be nice to see it open and running. One story that needs recalling is from March 1997, just after work started. They received a phone call: "I hope you are being careful with the U.X.B." (unexploded bomb) said the caller. Local radio, the Allan Beswick Show, took up the question, was there a U.X.B. there or not? They never found it, but it did slow them down for a week or two.

One part of the original plan for the Lowry Centre was for car parks on the Trafford Wharf and a bridge over to the Salford side to allow you to visit the centre. Above we see the stanchions of the bridge in place and ready for the walkway. Actually the photo was taken the morning that the walkway was to have been lowered into place, but it turned out to be too windy, and was postponed 24 hours. Below we see the bridge finally completed in February 1999, but what was to be the car park is now to be The Imperial War Museum of the North with work due to start on Jan 1st, 2000.

Loading fruit from the Middle East, at no. 8 dock sheds, on to a lorry for the Shude Hill Fruit and Veg Market, in the 1920's. Today it is the site of one of the gems of Salford Quays - 'The Heritage Project'. There are always good exhibitions on there and they are always friendly and helpful. Open Monday to Friday all year round the place is well worth a visit. And with all the millenium waterway plans just announced, flotillas from Castlefield basin. Ships setting out for the Millenium Dome, visiting ships etc, it will be a very busy place for the next few years.

St. Philip's Church, one of the hidden gems of Salford, above, on a picture taken only a few years ago. It was this church that had Rev Canon Peter Green as minister for so many years, 1911-51 after being rector of Sacred Trinity for ten years before that. You won't find anyone in Salford with anything but praise for that man and the church is almost his memorial.

Right we see the underneath of the railway arch that goes over Chapel St. Salford. The query keeps coming up about a statue that was once in the wall at this spot. Some say they remember it very worn and hard to make out what it was, while records and most books don't mention it at all, did it really exist? If you can help, write to be at the address on page two and help put many people out of their misery.

Bloom St. is a quiet backwater now, but was once one of the most important streets in Salford. Above we see the very imposing Salford Gas Offices there. I've promised not to mention the Salford Gas Scandal, so I won't, but look it up.

Left, we see the doorway of the King's Arms opposite. Salford has been proud of its royal connections and this must be one of the grandest entrances in the City. I went in recently and asked for half a lager. I received cold stares and the answer: "THIS IS A REAL ALE PUB". I had a half of whatever the special offer (visiting guest ale) was, and enjoyed it.

SALFORD CORPORATION

MODEL LODGING HOUSE

Everywhere I visited in Salford for research into this book I found growth, rebuilding, new life being breathed into run-down buildings and areas. Salford is looking forward. It just needs a centre to focus on, and forceful leadership. Salford Model Lodging House was built to give adequate accommodation to itinerant workers whilst in Salford. At one time over 100 workers could be given a clean bed for the night and safe shelter. It is now being turned into flats for young couples though as we see below there are still signs of the time it was a children's nursery.

Above we see the Farmer Norton factory on Adelphi St. being demolished. The heavy engineering firm had been there over a hundred years and made heaters and dryers for the textile industry. The firm closed in the 1980's, but what will rise on this spot? Below is the back of Salford Royal Hospital during its present "rejuvenation". The hospital had lain empty for many years before the present work turning it into a hotel started.

Salford pubs have had book after book written about them. The days when they would bet how far you could make it up Cross Lane or Regent Road having a half (they used to call it a gill) in every pub you came to. Now there are boarded up Inns, Hotels and pubs all over the city. Above we see what was a cosy and genteel watering hole just off Bexley Square. Below we see the most haunted pub in Salford. There are Spirits of the spooky sort in the cellar and upstairs where a jockey hung himself at the Griffin Hotel on the corner of Great Cheetham St. West and Lower Broughton Road.

The public baths in Collier Street, Salford, were opened by the Manchester and Salford Baths & Laundry Company Incorporated in 1855. The baths closed down in 1880 when the Salford Corporation opened their baths on Blackfriars St. on June 9th 1880. The building has had a very chequered history since then but it is still there today though what they are going to do with it is a big puzzle. Collier Street was named after Samuel Francis Collier, a hard working Methodist minister who did a lot for the poor and down trodden of that area.

Here we see two views of the inside of those baths. The male pool was the biggest and very ornately tiled while the smaller female bathing pool was tiled in plane white tiles. You can see above how the pools were built over when the building was being used as a match-box factory. Later an air-raid shelter was built at the deep end of the ladies' pool. Right you see the roof arches, and they were constructed of laminated wood built up of thin strips of wood and glued together. They were made long before the practice became widely used and are one of the reasons why the building should be preserved in some way.

The first new bridge to be built over the Irwell, between Salford and Manchester for a hundred years, was this footbridge which opened in September 1995. Dr. Santiago Calatrava was the Spanish architect who won the competition to design a footbridge between the two cities and that's how the bridge is now referred to - 'The Calatrava Bridge'. Above we see it from the Blackfriars Street bridge and right from the side of Albert Bridge House looking over to G.W.S. - God's Wonderful SALFORD.